PRAYERS

Kids

Special thanks to the fifth and sixth grade students at Victory Christian School in Niles, Ohio, and third through seventh grade Sunday school students at Cortland Trinity Baptist Church in Cortland, Ohio, for their contributions to this book.

© 2008 by Barbour Publishing, Inc.

Compiled by Rachel F. Overton.

ISBN 978-1-60260-195-6

Some material previously published in *Bible Answers for Preschoolers* and *31 Days with God for Grads*.

Scripture quotations marked NIV are taken from the HOLY BIBLE, NEW INTERNATIONAL VERSION® NIV®. Copyright © 1973, 1978, 1984 by International Bible Society. Used by permission of Zondervan. All rights reserved.

Scripture quotations marked NKJV are taken from the New King James Version®. Copyright © 1982 by Thomas Nelson, Inc. Used by permission. All rights reserved.

Scripture quotations marked MSG are taken from *THE MESSAGE*. Copyright © by Eugene H. Peterson 1993, 1994, 1995, 2000, 2001, 2002. Used by permission of NavPress Publishing Group.

Scripture quotations marked NLT are taken from the *Holy Bible*, New Living Translation, copyright 1996. Used by permission of Tyndale House Publishers, Inc. Wheaton, Illinois 60189, U.S.A. All rights reserved.

Published by Barbour Publishing, Inc., P.O. Box 719, Uhrichsville, Ohio 44683, www.barbourbooks.com

Our mission is to publish and distribute inspirational products offering exceptional value and biblical encouragement to the masses.

Member of the
Evangelical Christian
Publishers Association

Printed in China.

PRAYERS FOR
Kids

BARBOUR
PUBLISHING

GIVE YOURSELVES COMPLETELY TO GOD. . . .
USE YOUR WHOLE BODY AS AN INSTRUMENT
TO DO WHAT IS RIGHT FOR THE GLORY OF GOD.

ROMANS 6:13 NLT

God, sometimes the ideas
and dreams I have are so big, they scare me.
I know You made me the way I am for a reason.
Help me to know which dreams are part of Your plan.
Help me to choose what honors You. Amen.

Jesus, help me learn your word
so I can hide it in my heart.
When I can think of a Bible verse,
it reminds me that you're here,
even though I can't see you.
Amen.

Dear God,
thank You for making a home
for me in heaven.
Amen.

DEAR JESUS, SOME OF MY FRIENDS THINK BELIEVING IN YOU IS SILLY. HELP ME BE STRONG AND HONEST ABOUT HOW I FEEL ABOUT YOU. AMEN.

The main requirement for making a difference *for* Jesus is being in love *with* Jesus.

DAVE EARLEY

JESUS, HELP ME REMEMBER THAT JUST BECAUSE SOMEONE DOESN'T LOOK OR DRESS THE SAME WAY I DO, THAT DOESN'T MEAN I'M BETTER—OR WORSE—THAN THEY ARE. IT'S WHAT'S ON THE INSIDE THAT COUNTS. AMEN.

Dear Lord, thank You for sending Your Son
to be born, so He could die for my sins.
Amen.

DEAR LORD, THANK YOU FOR FREEDOM TO WORSHIP YOU.
I'M GLAD I CAN GO TO CHURCH AND TALK ABOUT
YOU AND NOT HAVE TO BE AFRAID THAT
SOMEONE WILL HURT ME OR PUT ME IN JAIL.
AMEN.

Dear God, thank You for the beautiful world
You have given us.
Amen.

I LOVE YOU, DEAR GOD.
AMEN.

Children, do what your parents tell you.
This is only right. "Honor your father and mother"
is the first commandment that has a promise attached to it,
namely, "so you will live well and have a long life."

EPHESIANS 6:1-3 MSG

Jesus, I know I'm supposed to honor my parents,
but sometimes I don't.
I'm sorry for not obeying you
and for disrespecting my parents.
Please help me do better.
Amen.

Lord, I want to hear from You today in a special way.
Open my eyes and my heart.
Lead me in Your scripture to words meant just for me.
Amen.

Jesus, help me remember to look to you for answers, not my friends or other people around me. Amen.

Dear God, when someone hurts my feelings,
I need Your help to forgive them.
And when I make a mistake,
thank You for forgiving me!
Amen.

FATHER, I DON'T KNOW HOW YOU WILL USE MY LIFE,
BUT I HAVE FAITH IN YOUR PROMISES AND
AM ALWAYS READY TO DO YOUR WILL.
AMEN.

Every person you meet knows something you don't.
Learn from them.

H. JACKSON BROWN JR.

THANK YOU, LORD, FOR SAVING ME FROM MYSELF.
AMEN.

God, sometimes I don't want to be good.
Sometimes I want to do the things my friends do—
the things that are against my parents' rules.
I've always said I loved You and wanted to be like You,
but it's getting harder to do that.
Help me to do what is right.
Amen.

DEAR GOD, MY HOPE IS IN YOU AND YOUR PROMISES.
THANK YOU FOR BEING SO GOOD TO ME.
AMEN.

Dear God, it's hard to be patient.
Please help me wait with a smile on my face.
Amen.

FATHER, WHEN MY LIFE TURNS UPSIDE DOWN,
I WILL TRUST YOU TO LEAD ME IN THE RIGHT DIRECTION.
AMEN.

Jesus, if You were able to feed more than five thousand people
with just five loaves of bread and two fish,
I know You can meet all my needs.
Help me to trust You to take care of me.
Amen.

IF YOU CONFESS WITH YOUR MOUTH, "JESUS IS LORD,"
AND BELIEVE IN YOUR HEART THAT GOD RAISED HIM
FROM THE DEAD, YOU WILL BE SAVED.

ROMANS 10:9 NIV

Dear God, I'm so glad I can talk to You.
You always hear my prayers.
Thank You for loving me so much.
Amen.

DEAR GOD, THANK YOU FOR ALL THE GOOD THINGS
YOU GIVE ME. I LOVE YOU, GOD.
AMEN.

Jesus, help me be brave when other kids tease me
because I'm not like them.
I'm different because I belong to You.
Amen.

JESUS, WHEN I GET MAD AND WANT TO YELL
OR HURT SOMEONE, PLEASE GIVE ME SELF-CONTROL
SO I WON'T DO ANYTHING STUPID.
AMEN.

Dear God, please give our president wisdom.
He has lots of decisions to make and lots of people
who don't like what he decides, no matter what it is.
Please help him be smart and strong.
Keep him safe and help Him to remember
that You are really in charge.
Amen.

THERE ARE MANY THINGS IN LIFE THAT WILL CATCH YOUR EYE,
BUT ONLY A FEW WILL CATCH YOUR HEART—PURSUE THOSE.

UNKNOWN

Father, I want to follow in Your path.
Help me listen and know when You're talking to me
so I can know which way to go.
Amen.

JESUS, HELP ME SEE WHEN MY FRIENDS ARE HURT
OR SAD SO I CAN SHARE YOUR LOVE WITH THEM.
AMEN.

Father God, I know You love me
and that You will protect me.
Thank You.
Amen.

YOU WILL SEEK ME AND FIND ME
WHEN YOU SEEK ME WITH ALL YOUR HEART.

JEREMIAH 29:13 NIV

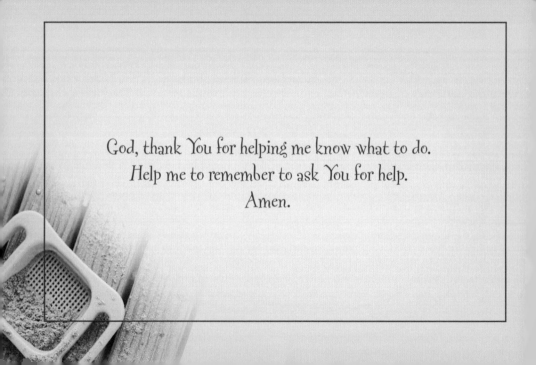

God, thank You for helping me know what to do.
Help me to remember to ask You for help.
Amen.

JESUS, I'M GLAD YOU LIVED ON EARTH LIKE ME.
YOU KNOW WHAT IT FEELS LIKE
TO BE HAPPY AND SAD AND MAD.
IT HELPS ME WHEN I REMEMBER YOUR EXAMPLE.
AMEN.

Thank You, Jesus, that when I tell
You about things I do wrong,
You forgive me and I can start all over again.
I'm glad You love me enough to do that!
Help me be like You.
Amen.

JESUS, THANK YOU FOR MY MOM.
HELP ME FIND SPECIAL WAYS TO LET
HER KNOW THAT I APPRECIATE HER.
AMEN.

Always be a first-rate version of yourself,
instead of a second-rate version of somebody else.

JUDY GARLAND

LORD, I DID IT AGAIN. I TRY SO HARD TO DO THINGS RIGHT,
BUT THEN I DON'T. HELP ME REMEMBER THAT
MY STRENGTH COMES FROM YOU, NOT ME.
THANK YOU FOR FORGIVING ME EVERY TIME I MESS UP,
EVEN WHEN I DO THE SAME THINGS OVER AND OVER.
AMEN.

God, I know You command us to love everyone,
but it's hard to love the people I don't like!
Help me to see these people with Your eyes
and love them with Your heart.
Amen.

DEAR JESUS, THANK YOU FOR FILLING
MY HEART WITH YOUR LOVE.
I LOVE YOU.
AMEN.

Jesus, sometimes my mom and dad
have some grown-up problems
I don't understand,
but You know how to fix things.
Please help them today.
Amen.

DEAR GOD, HELP ME TO REMEMBER THAT
EVERYTHING I HAVE IS A GIFT FROM YOU.
HELP ME SHARE THESE GIFTS WITH OTHERS.
AMEN.

Even a child is known by his actions,
by whether his conduct is pure and right.

PROVERBS 20:11 NIV

GOD, I WANT TO STAND UP FOR WHAT I BELIEVE,
BUT I'M AFRAID OF WHAT PEOPLE WILL THINK
OR SAY ABOUT ME. HELP ME TO STAND,
UNASHAMED, FOR WHAT I KNOW IS RIGHT.
AMEN.

Dear Jesus, thank You for my dad.
He's great!
Amen.

DEAR GOD, THANK YOU FOR KEEPING YOUR PROMISES.
AMEN.

Dear God, I never need to feel alone.
You are always here to make me feel safe and special.
You love me—the Bible tells me so!
Amen.

WHAT YOU ARE IS GOD'S GIFT TO YOU.
WHAT YOU MAKE OF YOURSELF IS YOUR GIFT BACK TO GOD.

KELLY JEPPESEN

Jesus, I know You choose people to do special
things for You, but I don't feel special.
I know You can use me to do great things.
Here I am. I'm Yours.
Amen.

JESUS, I WANT YOU TO USE ME TO TELL MY FRIENDS ABOUT YOU.
PLEASE SHOW ME OPPORTUNITIES TO DO THAT.
AMEN.

Lord, I know You can do the impossible.
Would You, please?
Amen.

THANK YOU, LORD, FOR TODAY.
I WANT TO MAKE THE MOST OF IT
BY SHOWING SOMEONE YOUR LOVE.
AMEN.

Dear Lord, I pray for the soldiers who are away
from home and fighting so we can be safe here.
Please protect them, and if they don't know You,
send someone to tell them about You.
Amen.

ANYONE WHO BELONGS TO CHRIST
HAS BECOME A NEW PERSON.
THE OLD LIFE IS GONE; A NEW LIFE HAS BEGUN!

2 CORINTHIANS 5:17 NLT

God, please help me learn to know Your voice
and be able to tell the difference when Satan
tries to tell me something that isn't true.
Amen.

THANK YOU, GOD, THAT YOU GIVE ME
THE STRENGTH TO DO ANYTHING FOR YOU.
AMEN.

Lord, I'm so glad that You love me even though
You know everything about me—even the bad stuff.
Thank You for Your unconditional love.
Amen.

FATHER GOD, THANK YOU FOR GIVING
ME EVERYTHING I NEED.
YOU ARE SO GOOD TO ME.
AMEN.

Jesus, thank You that You never change.
Amen.

TO DREAM OF THE PERSON YOU'D LIKE TO BE
IS TO WASTE THE PERSON YOU ARE.

UNKNOWN

Jesus, sometimes my life gets crazy.
Help me remember that You're in control
and You know what's going to happen before I do.
I'm going to trust You to keep me safe.
Amen.

GOD, MY DAD IS SO GREAT.
HE WORKS REALLY HARD SO THAT WE
CAN HAVE ALL THE THINGS WE HAVE.
SOMETIMES HE GETS REALLY TIRED, THOUGH.
HELP ME KNOW HOW TO MAKE HIM FEEL BETTER
WHEN HE'S DOWN.
AMEN.

Dear Jesus, please help me remember all the things
I studied and heard in class.
Amen.

LORD, HELP ME TO BE A GOOD FRIEND.
HELP ME TREAT PEOPLE FAIRLY AND HONESTLY.
HELP ME TO SHOW LOVE, EVEN WHEN
THE OTHER PERSON HURTS MY FEELINGS.
AMEN.

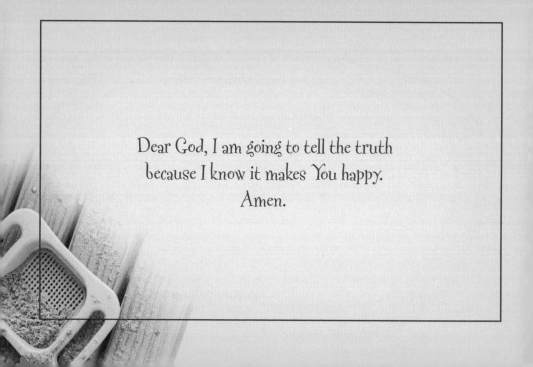

Dear God, I am going to tell the truth
because I know it makes You happy.
Amen.

FOR GOD SO LOVED THE WORLD THAT HE GAVE HIS ONE AND ONLY SON, THAT WHOEVER BELIEVES IN HIM SHALL NOT PERISH BUT HAVE ETERNAL LIFE.

JOHN 3:16 NIV

Dear Jesus, why are friends mean sometimes?
My friend really hurt my feelings,
but Mom says I need to forgive him.
Help me do that.
Amen.

IT IS SO PRETTY OUTSIDE, GOD.
THANKS FOR SUNSHINE AND
NICE WEATHER SO I CAN PLAY.
AMEN.

I want to be a strong Christian, Lord, not a pretender.
Help me live for You in every way.
Amen.

GOD, HELP ME HONOR MY PARENTS.
AMEN.

How I look is not as important as how I act.

LEAH DAVIES

GOD, HELP ME NOT JUDGE PEOPLE BY HOW THEY LOOK. HELP ME SEE WHO'S INSIDE, NOT JUST THEIR CLOTHES OR THEIR SIZE OR HOW PRETTY THEY ARE. HELP ME SEE PEOPLE THE WAY YOU DO—NOT THE WAY OTHER PEOPLE DO.

AMEN.

Jesus, I belong to You.
I want to do what You want me to do.
Show me Your will.
Amen.

HEAVENLY FATHER, THANK YOU FOR SHOWING
ME YOU LOVE ME IN GREAT BIG WAYS
AND IN LITTLE TINY DETAILS, TOO.
AMEN.

Dear God, sometimes my family makes me so mad!
But I still love them.
Help me to have patience with them.
Amen.

CHILDREN, OBEY YOUR PARENTS IN EVERYTHING,
FOR THIS PLEASES THE LORD.

COLOSSIANS 3:20 NIV

Jesus, some of my friends don't know You.
Help me show them that You love them
and that You want to live in their hearts, too.
Amen.

I DON'T UNDERSTAND YOUR WAYS, GOD,
AND MY HEART DOESN'T ALWAYS BELIEVE
WHAT I KNOW WITH MY HEAD—
THAT YOU ARE ALWAYS DOING GOOD.
HELP ME TRUST YOU MORE.
AMEN.

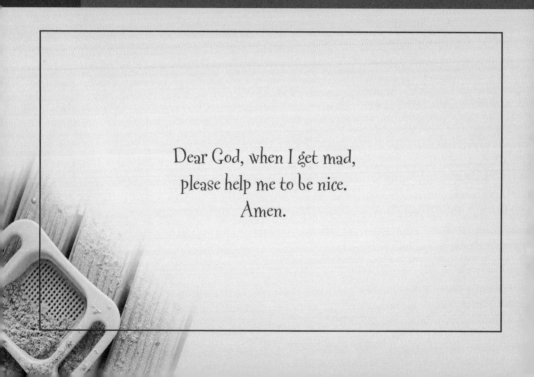

Dear God, when I get mad,
please help me to be nice.
Amen.

DEAR GOD, I HAVE FAITH IN YOUR PROMISES.
I KNOW IF YOU SAY IT, YOU WILL DO IT.
AMEN.

God, Your Word tells me that I have been set apart as holy.
Show me the ways in my life You want me
to be different from others around me.
Amen.

CHARACTER IS MADE BY WHAT YOU STAND FOR;
REPUTATION BY WHAT YOU FALL FOR.

BRUCE BICKEL & STAN JANTZ

Jesus, thank You for being a good example of how to obey.
You did what Your Father wanted,
even though it meant You had to die on a cross.
Thank You for dying for me and for rising again
so I could be a child of God.
Help me to be obedient, too.
Amen.

GOD, SOMETIMES I'M AFRAID OF THE DARK.
MOM SAYS THE BIBLE IS A LIGHT FOR ME,
SO COULD YOU MAKE IT LIGHT IN MY HEART,
EVEN IF IT'S DARK AROUND ME?
AMEN.

Dear Jesus, thank You for pets.
They show Your love in a different way
than humans, and I like it!
Amen.

LORD, HELP ME TO LISTEN TODAY.
AMEN.

"I know the plans I have for you," declares the LORD,
"plans to prosper you and not to harm you,
plans to give you hope and a future."

JEREMIAH 29:11 NIV

EVERYTHING GOOD COMES FROM YOU, LORD.
AND EVERYTHING YOU DO IS GOOD.
HELP ME TO REMEMBER THAT EVEN WHEN
THINGS LOOK BAD AND SCARY.
I KNOW EVERYTHING WILL WORK OUT OKAY
BECAUSE YOU LOVE ME.
AMEN.

Dear God, thank You for my friends.
Help me to always treat them just the way
I want to be treated.
Amen.

Jesus, I want to live my life in a way that shows you to the people around me.
Amen.

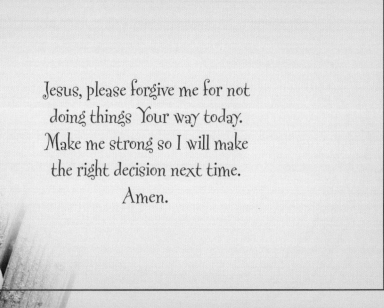

Jesus, please forgive me for not
doing things Your way today.
Make me strong so I will make
the right decision next time.
Amen.

FATHER GOD, FILL ME WITH YOUR LOVE FOR OTHERS.
AMEN.

There are wonders in prayer
because there are wonders in God.

E. M. BOUNDS

GOD, I'M THANKFUL THAT YOUR LOVE
IS BIG ENOUGH FOR THE WHOLE WORLD.
AMEN.

God, I'm glad You sent the Holy Spirit to live inside me.
I know He's there all the time,
and the Bible says He talks to You for me,
even when I don't know what to say.
That's cool!
Amen.

GOD, FORGIVING SOMEONE WHO'S
HURT ME IS REALLY HARD TO DO.
PLEASE HELP ME FORGIVE COMPLETELY,
THE WAY YOU'VE FORGIVEN ME.
AMEN.

Dear God, I'm glad You gave me patient parents.
They must be a lot like You.
Amen.

NO TEST OR TEMPTATION THAT COMES YOUR WAY
IS BEYOND THE COURSE OF WHAT OTHERS HAVE HAD TO FACE.
ALL YOU NEED TO REMEMBER IS THAT GOD WILL NEVER LET
YOU DOWN; HE'LL NEVER LET YOU BE PUSHED PAST YOUR LIMIT;
HE'LL ALWAYS BE THERE TO HELP YOU COME THROUGH IT.

1 CORINTHIANS 10:13 MSG

Jesus, sometimes it's hard to find good role models.
Please bring people into my life that love You
and honor You in all they do.
Amen.

DEAR GOD, I WANT TO BE KIND,
SHOWING YOUR LOVE TO OTHERS EVERY DAY.
AMEN.

Dear God, thank You for taking my worries away.
Amen.

GOD, I'M JUST A KID, BUT SHOW ME
SOMETHING I CAN DO THAT WILL MAKE
A DIFFERENCE IN SOMEONE ELSE'S LIFE.
AMEN.

To be yourself in a world that is constantly trying to make you something else is the greatest accomplishment.

RALPH WALDO EMERSON

JESUS, HELP ME CHOOSE MY FRIENDS WISELY.
I KNOW THAT THE PEOPLE I HANG OUT
WITH ARE THE PEOPLE I WILL ACT LIKE,
SO HELP ME CHOOSE FRIENDS WHO
WON'T ENCOURAGE ME TO BE BAD.
AMEN.

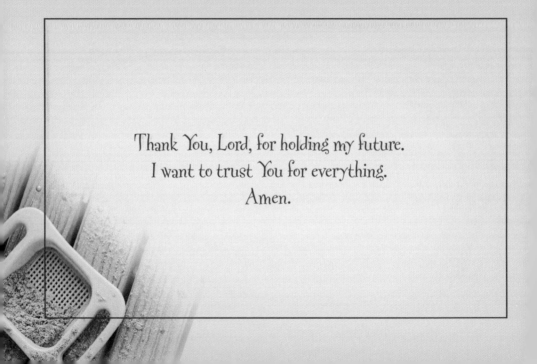

Thank You, Lord, for holding my future.
I want to trust You for everything.
Amen.

DEAR GOD, PLEASE HELP THE CHILDREN
AND GROWN-UPS WHO DON'T HAVE ANYTHING
AND ARE STARVING IN OTHER COUNTRIES.
AMEN.

Dear God, I just love Christmas.
It is one of my favorite times of year.
But I just can't stop thinking about the presents!
This Christmas, I want to think about Jesus' birthday.
Thank You for sending Your Son to us.
Amen.

DEAR LORD, PLEASE HELP MY FAMILY
COME TO KNOW YOU BETTER.
AMEN.

Jesus...said to them,
"Let the little children come to Me,
and do not forbid them;
for of such is the kingdom of God."

MARK 10:14 NKJV

DEAR JESUS, I PRAY FOR THE PEOPLE WHO ARE HOMELESS
AND DON'T HAVE JOBS OR MONEY OR FOOD.
HELP PEOPLE WHO HAVE LOTS TO SHARE
WITH THEM AND NOT TREAT THEM BAD.
HELP THEM LEARN ABOUT YOU, TOO.
AMEN.

Dear Jesus, please help all the people who are sick.
And be with their families and help them
know that You are there for them.
Amen.

DEAR LORD, PLEASE HELP ME STOP MAKING FUN OF
OTHER PEOPLE. I KNOW I'M NOT SO NICE SOMETIMES,
AND I DON'T WANT TO BE THAT WAY ANYMORE.
AMEN.

Dear God, please let me be a light for You in dark places. Amen.

DEAR GOD, THANK YOU FOR SNOW.
I LOVE TO PLAY IN IT.
AMEN.

Never let the fear of striking out
keep you from playing the game.

A CINDERELLA STORY

GOD, SOMETIMES I FEEL LIKE I DON'T HAVE
ANY TALENT AT ALL, BUT I KNOW THAT CAN'T
BE TRUE BECAUSE YOU HAVE A PLAN FOR ME.
HELP ME FIND THE THINGS I'M GOOD AT
AND LEARN TO USE THEM FOR YOU.
I WANT TO HONOR YOU WITH
THE WAY YOU MADE ME.
AMEN.

Dear God, sometimes the evening news has scary reports
of people who want to hurt others.
Help me to remember that You are in control,
and You will keep me safe from harm.
Amen.

DEAR GOD, PLEASE BE WITH THE SOLDIERS
WHO ARE FIGHTING FOR OUR COUNTRY.
IF THEY'RE SAD AND SCARED, PLEASE COMFORT THEM.
PLEASE KEEP THEM SAFE AND HELP THEM TRUST YOU.
AND BRING THEM BACK HOME QUICKLY.
AMEN.

Dear Lord, thank You for giving me a great school
where I can spend my days learning lots.
Amen.

DEAR GOD, SOMETIMES I GET SCARED AT NIGHT.
PLEASE HELP ME GO TO SLEEP QUICKLY
SO I WON'T BE AFRAID AND HAVE BAD DREAMS.
AMEN.

I have hidden your word in my heart
that I might not sin against you.

PSALM 119:11 NIV

DEAR LORD, I PRAY FOR MY MINISTER AND HIS FAMILY.
HELP THEM BE STRONG AND LIVE FOR YOU.
KEEP THEM SAFE AND PROTECT THEM
FROM SATAN'S ATTACKS.
BLESS THEM FOR SERVING YOU.
AMEN.

God, sometimes I'm afraid to go to school.
It's supposed to be a safe place, but it isn't always.
Please keep my school safe and help me concentrate
and not be afraid.
Amen.

DEAR GOD, PLEASE HELP ME BE MORE SERIOUS
ABOUT STUDYING AND DOING MY HOMEWORK.
EVERYTHING I DO IS A REFLECTION OF YOU,
SO HELP ME WANT TO DO MY BEST.
AMEN.

Dear God, I want to keep my heart
and my thoughts pure.
Amen.

DEAR LORD, I WANT PEOPLE TO KNOW
WHY I'M DIFFERENT—BECAUSE I LOVE YOU
AND I AM YOUR CHILD.
AMEN.

Dear God, I pray for our country,
that we won't forget You.
Amen.

DEAR JESUS, I KNOW YOU WANT EVERYONE
TO GO TO HEAVEN, SO I WILL OBEY
AND TELL THEM ABOUT YOU.
AMEN.

The LORD is my light
and my salvation—whom shall I fear?
The LORD is the stronghold of my life—
of whom shall I be afraid?

PSALM 27:1 NIV

DEAR GOD, PLEASE HELP MY TEACHERS.
IT CAN'T ALWAYS BE EASY TO PUT UP WITH
THE KIDS IN MY CLASS.
AMEN.

Dear Jesus, I don't have a lot of money,
but I want to help people who are in need.
Show me how I can.
Amen.

DEAR GOD, HELP ME TO BE HAPPY
WITH THE WAY YOU MADE ME.
AMEN.

Thank You, Jesus, for Your Word.
Help me want to spend more time reading it,
instead of always watching TV or doing other things
that don't bring me closer to You.
Amen.

GOD, THANK YOU FOR MY GRANDPARENTS
AND AUNTS AND UNCLES AND COUSINS.
THEY ARE SPECIAL TO ME.
AMEN.

Thank You, Jesus, for Your grace.
You've done everything that had to be done
to bring me into heaven.
All I had to do was accept Your gift.
Wow! I want to give You my life as thanks.
Amen.

WHEN WE WORK, WE WORK.
BUT WHEN WE PRAY, GOD WORKS.

BILL HYBELS

Dear God, I pray for the missionaries in other countries.
Please keep them safe and help them
to tell the people around them about You.
I pray that lots of people will listen and believe.
Amen.

DEAR GOD, SOMETIMES IT'S HARD TO TELL
WHAT IS TRUTH AND WHAT IS A LIE.
PLEASE HELP ME TO REMEMBER TO GO TO
YOUR WORD TO FIND THE REAL TRUTH.
AMEN.

Use what talents you possess—
the woods would be very silent if no birds sang
except those that sang the best.

HENRY VAN DYKE

JESUS, SOMETIMES I GET REALLY SAD AND DEPRESSED,
BUT I FEEL FUNNY TELLING ANYONE ABOUT IT.
PLEASE GIVE ME A PERSON I CAN TALK TO ABOUT THIS.
AMEN.

Dear God, whatever I do when I grow up, I want to do Your will.
Please show me what career You want me to have
so that I can glorify You.
Amen.

FAILURE IS NOT THE FALLING DOWN,
BUT THE STAYING DOWN.

MARY PICKFORD

Dear Lord, thank You for putting people in the world
who stand up for other people.
Amen.

JESUS, SOMETIMES MY MOUTH SAYS THINGS
BEFORE I EVEN REALIZE THE WORDS ARE HURTFUL.
PLEASE HELP ME TO TAME MY TONGUE
AND THINK BEFORE I SPEAK.
AMEN.

Your hands made me and formed me;
give me understanding to learn your commands.

DEAR LORD, THANK YOU FOR PUTTING
ME ON THIS EARTH FOR A REASON,
EVEN IF I DON'T KNOW WHAT IT IS YET.
YOU KNOW, AND YOU WILL HELP ME KNOW
WHEN IT'S TIME. I CAN'T WAIT TO FIND OUT.
AMEN.

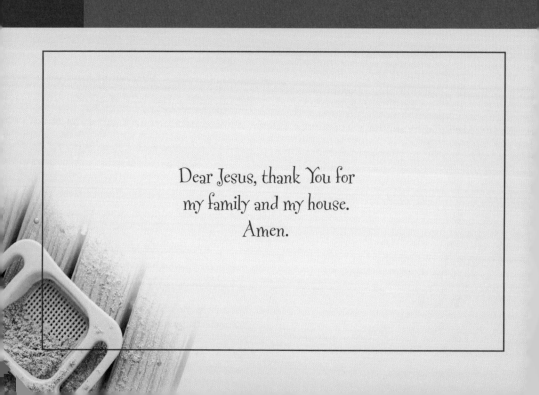

Dear Jesus, thank You for
my family and my house.
Amen.

DEAR GOD, I WANT TO OBEY YOUR WORD
EVERY DAY IN EVERYTHING I DO.
AMEN.

Dear God, please help the people
in other countries who are suffering.
I pray they'll have somewhere safe to sleep
and enough food to eat tonight.
Amen.

DEAR JESUS, HELP ME KNOW WHICH PEOPLE
I CAN TRUST AND WHICH ONES I SHOULDN'T.
KEEP ME SAFE FROM PEOPLE WHO
MIGHT WANT TO HURT ME.
AMEN.

No one can make you feel inferior without your consent.

ELEANOR ROOSEVELT

FOR I AM CONVINCED THAT NEITHER DEATH NOR LIFE,
NEITHER ANGELS NOR DEMONS, NEITHER THE PRESENT
NOR THE FUTURE, NOR ANY POWERS, NEITHER HEIGHT
NOR DEPTH, NOR ANYTHING ELSE IN ALL CREATION,
WILL BE ABLE TO SEPARATE US FROM THE LOVE
OF GOD THAT IS IN CHRIST JESUS OUR LORD.

ROMANS 8:38–39 NIV

God, I'm glad I don't have to be perfect to be Your child.

I'm glad You sent Jesus—who is perfect!—

to die for me so I could be with You.

You're amazing, God.

Amen.

DEAR GOD, BLESS MOM AND DAD TODAY.
THEY WORK SO HARD TO KEEP OUR FAMILY SAFE
AND WARM AND FED AND LOVED.
THANK YOU FOR MY SPECIAL PARENTS.
AMEN.

Dear God, thank You for America.
We're strong because we believed in You,
but not everyone does anymore.
Please help Christians be brave
and stand up for what's right
so our country can stay free.
Amen.

DEAR HEAVENLY FATHER, I PRAY THAT I WILL GROW UP
TO BE THE PERSON YOU WANT ME TO BE.
PLEASE HELP ME TO BE KIND, GENEROUS, AND LOVING.
I WANT TO KNOW YOU BETTER EACH DAY
OF MY LIFE. I LOVE YOU.
AMEN.

A day without laughter is a day wasted.

CHARLIE CHAPLIN

DEAR GOD, THANK YOU FOR MY PETS.
PLEASE KEEP THEM SAFE AND HEALTHY.
AMEN.

Dear Lord, thank You for my church and my pastors
and my teachers who love You and tell others about You.
Help me be like them.
Amen.

DEAR JESUS, I PRAY FOR THE KIDS WHO DON'T
KNOW YOU AND WHO THINK NO ONE LOVES THEM.
YOU LOVE THEM, JESUS, I KNOW YOU DO.
SO PLEASE HELP THEM FIND OUT ABOUT YOU.
AMEN.

Lord, the world is so exciting.
It's so full of things to see and do and learn.
Some of them are good and some are not.
Help me to make choices that will honor You
and not take me away from You.
Amen.

JESUS CHRIST IS THE SAME YESTERDAY
AND TODAY AND FOREVER.

HEBREWS 13:8 NIV

Dear God, I want to appreciate what I have and not be jealous when someone else has something (or lots of things) that I want. I want to build up treasures in heaven, not on earth. I know You give me what I need, so help me remember that things are just stuff, and they mean nothing in heaven. Amen.

Jesus, I want the way I live to make you happy.
Amen.

Dear God, thank You for helping and comforting me through the times that I need it.
Amen.

RIGHT IS RIGHT, EVEN IF EVERYONE IS AGAINST IT;
AND WRONG IS WRONG, EVEN IF EVERYONE IS FOR IT.

WILLIAM PENN

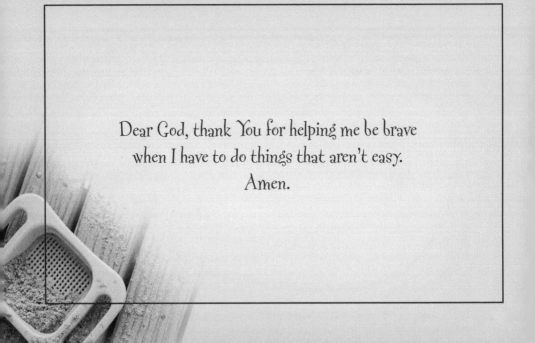

Dear God, thank You for helping me be brave
when I have to do things that aren't easy.
Amen.

DEAR GOD, THANK YOU FOR PROTECTING ME.
BECAUSE YOU ARE ALWAYS WITH ME,
I DON'T EVER HAVE TO BE AFRAID OF ANYTHING.
AMEN.

Dear Lord, help me be brave and honest with my parents.
I've been doing some things that I know
are wrong and I want to stop.
Telling my parents will make me accountable
and make it harder to keep doing it.
Help them not be too angry
or disappointed in me.
Amen.

DEAR GOD, PLEASE HELP ME LOVE OTHERS
AS MUCH AS YOU LOVE ME.
AMEN.

Dear Lord, I thank You for all that You have given me.
Please help others who don't have as much
and who are going through hard times.
Amen.

O LORD, YOU ARE SO GOOD, SO READY TO FORGIVE,
SO FULL OF UNFAILING LOVE FOR ALL
WHO ASK FOR YOUR HELP.

PSALM 86:5 NLT

Dear God, thank You for coming
to my rescue when I'm hurt.
You always know just what I need
when I'm feeling down.
Amen.

DEAR GOD, HELP ME NOT BE SELFISH.
AMEN.

Dear Jesus, I don't like it when kids pick on other kids.

I don't want to be like that.

I'm going to be like You

and love everyone, no matter what.

Amen.

HITCH YOUR WAGON TO A STAR.

RALPH WALDO EMERSON

God, sometimes it drives me crazy that I'm not in control!
Help me to remember that
You've got the future all planned out,
so I don't have to worry about anything!
Amen.

DEAR LORD, THANKS FOR ALL THE
THINGS YOU HAVE GIVEN ME.
AMEN.

Dear Lord, thank You that our country is safe.
Amen.

JESUS, I DON'T DESERVE YOUR LOVE,
BUT I SURE AM HAPPY TO HAVE IT.
I KNOW I'LL NEVER BE PERFECT,
BUT I WANT TO LIVE WORTHY OF YOUR LOVE.
AMEN.

DEAR GOD, THANK YOU FOR A MOM AND DAD
WHO LOVE YOU AND TEACH ME ABOUT YOU.
AMEN.

Many, O LORD my God, are the wonders you have done.
The things you planned for us no one can recount to you;
were I to speak and tell of them,
they would be too many to declare.

PSALM 40:5 NIV

YOU WILL KEEP IN PERFECT PEACE
HIM WHOSE MIND IS STEADFAST,
BECAUSE HE TRUSTS IN YOU.

ISAIAH 26:3 NIV

Father, thank You that even though my words
don't always come out right when I pray,
You know what my heart means.
Sometimes people misunderstand me,
but You never do. I'm glad!
Amen.